cells

Lucianna Chixaro Ramos

bp

BURROW PRESS | ORLANDO, FL

Cells © Lucianna Chixaro Ramos, 2023
Cover illustration: Robert Hooke, from *Micrographia*, 1665
Cover design: Lucianna Chixaro Ramos
Book design: Ryan Rivas
Published by Burrow Press
burrowpress.com
All rights reserved.
POD Edition.
ISBN: 978-1-941681-25-1

Praise for *Cells*

Though "Healing cannot be / produced by a single / member of the colony" Lucianna Chixaro Ramos' breathtaking—breath-giving—debut collection offers an effective way forward into the kind of embodied and collective emotional intelligence that brings better health. Moving with exquisite grace and energy from micro(scope) to macro insight, letting language's limitations as an investigative tool reveal themselves, *Cells* is a sure, spacious, and exciting exploration of countries, institutions, boundaries, horizons—all the social, perceptual, and physical "structures that build us [and] contain us." I love Chixaro Ramos' *Cells* for the care the author takes with frameworks (always under question), the unfailingly tender and true grasp of attention's timing, and her approach to the philosophical, economic, and literary questions she is asking: an approach that is erudite, grounded, and aware of "a larger world." Quietly revolutionary, nourishingly radical: "If it no longer matters to be / quiet, compliant // then"—this book is for you.

—LAURA MULLEN **author of** *Complicated Grief*

The composer John Cage was famous for saying that art should imitate nature in its manner of operation. Ramos's *Cells* questions and complicates that idea, presenting the beehive as a trope for all sorts of thorny constraints and limitations—in the workplace, at national borders, within economic models, in poetic form itself. In our various cells, must we always serve a Queen? Must we forever have a Keeper? If so, how can we break free? This stunning collection urges us to imagine more nourishing forms of life.

—JENA OSMAN **author of** *Motion Studies*

What a pleasure to watch this gorgeous book build out. One tiny example: the semantic kink between sting/sing critiqued in a title ("Inequality II"). Plus the parentheses (pulled apart cell curves?) surrounding/broken by that title. Always, then, with Lucianna Chixaro Ramos' dry, delicate reasoning. Always in lines plush with the satisfyingly rich, unregulated research of a true buzzy-brain. Plus what meticulous page making—as visual poetry cells, these black/white forms are swerves and holders, counter-page planets. What's a book of poetry, exactly? *Cells* never falls into suspect "superorganism" status or becomes its own self-extraction device; rather, it expands into a half-hidden and raging thing called "queen" that's not quite the poet. Something monstrous called "Keeper"—also not quite the poet. Each, like (text) and (image) here, "selectively permeable." What a debut. Ouch.

—TERRI WITEK **author of** *Something's Missing in the Museum*

Table of Contents

I.

Hooke & the Bees

(Under the Microscope)

In 1665 Robert Hooke described the cells in a thin slice of cork:
an empty honey-comb, a wool, a sponge, a pumice stone,

a counterintuitive substance. Full of air, yet tough
as concrete, a cavern, a bubble. Then came a perceptive shift:

There is always, hanging over us, the possibility
that things previously invisible form the very structures

that build us. That contain us. And how can we know?
And how can we know that we know? In the end,

there is an attempt to be humble as cork. Hooke stands tentatively
on his own unknown, that infinite tightrope, *ready to be corrected.*

*

Hooke described a Terra Incognita
in his *Micrographia*. It bears repeating:

there is always, hanging over us, the possibility
that things previously invisible form
the very structures that build us. That contain us.

This possibility points to the likelihood of confinement.
The period at the end of a sentence.

*

In 1665, man coined the *cell*, a term that describes more
than its biology. He revealed a weapon of offense in diminutive
(read: feminine) form.

Aside from cork, Hooke observed many other objects:
the poppy seed's hexagonal chambers, a fish's scales
(up-close flowers in bloom), and even the moon,

though he concedes, only *a small spot of it*.

Amid this odd collection lies the sting of the common bee
which Hooke meticulously engraved, rendering each detail
from the puberulous, bulbous end, to the barbed tip, lettered 'a.'

Of this, Hooke wrote that *nature did really intend revenge
for there is no other use of it*. The sting, like a cat's claw
or a fish's scales, now made an admirable structure.

The minute body of it, like our minute bodies, scrutinized,
observed. In it, our weapons, our rage, barbed and lettered.
So commonplace, its appearance *need not be described.*

If you haven't seen it, you must not have looked close enough.

*

The moment man discovered cells in the cork,
it was discovered we are not who we are without confinement.

The shape of a life, a sentence, a poem, is drawn
by those who can operate within its constraints, manipulate them.

Is there anything outside this?

II.

Membranes

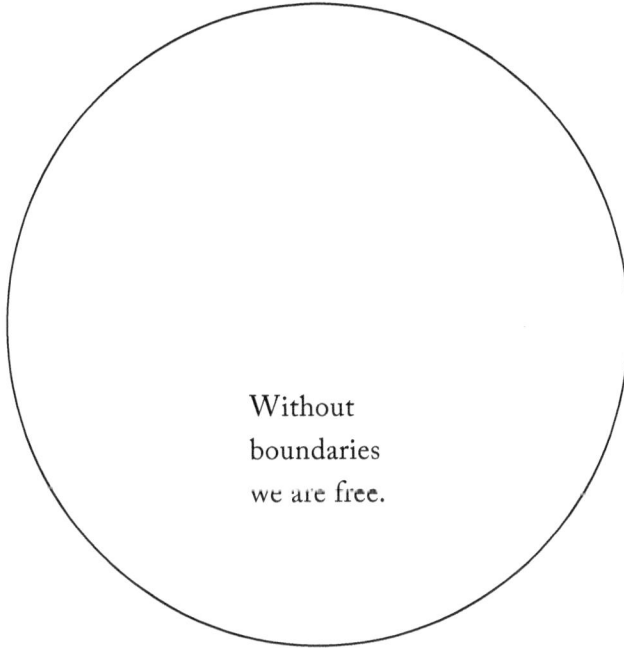

Without
boundaries
we are free.

Total
freedom is
counter to
production.

Skin is a boundary—
cells are—

organelles
within cells are—

atoms—
this negative space—

Sentences—

phrases—

words—

strokes—

poems are—

What is it we cannot yet see?

Are there a select few

who can see these structures

and extend beyond them?

Without order/s there are no results.

Without structure there is no body.

Nobody.

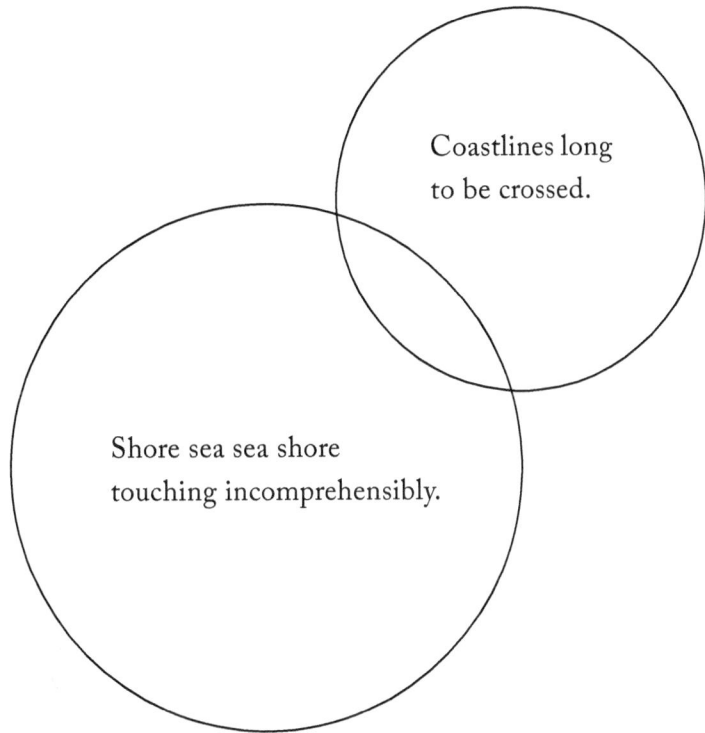

Coastlines long
to be crossed.

Shore sea sea shore
touching incomprehensibly.

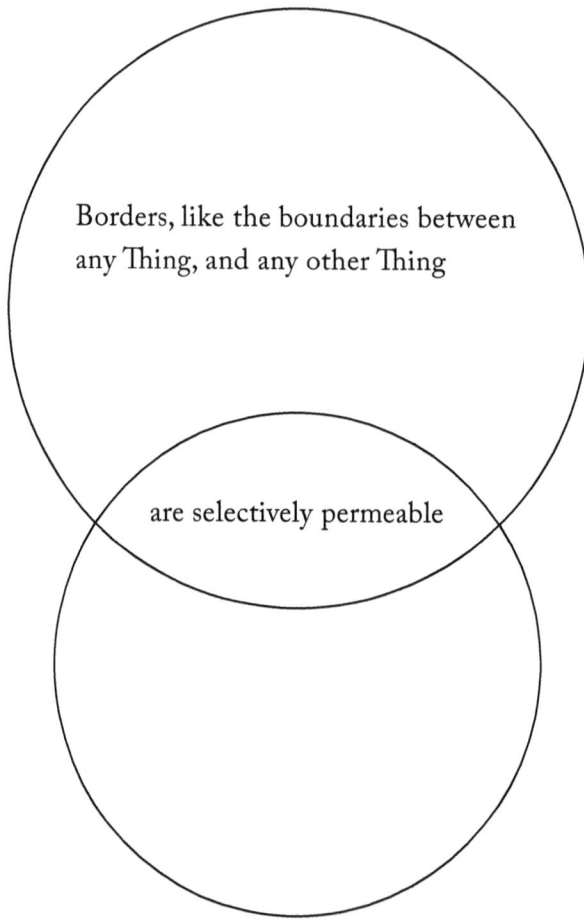

Borders, like the boundaries between any Thing, and any other Thing

are selectively permeable

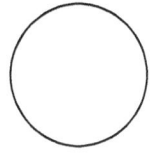

A cell is not just a set of boundaries.
It is a participatory body.

Its miniscule parts are a complex machinery
of vesicles, apparatuses, microtubules, and membranes.

Each is a working member occupying a larger world.

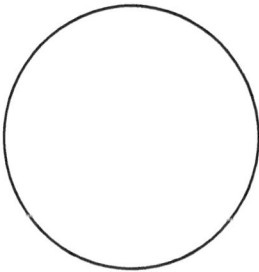

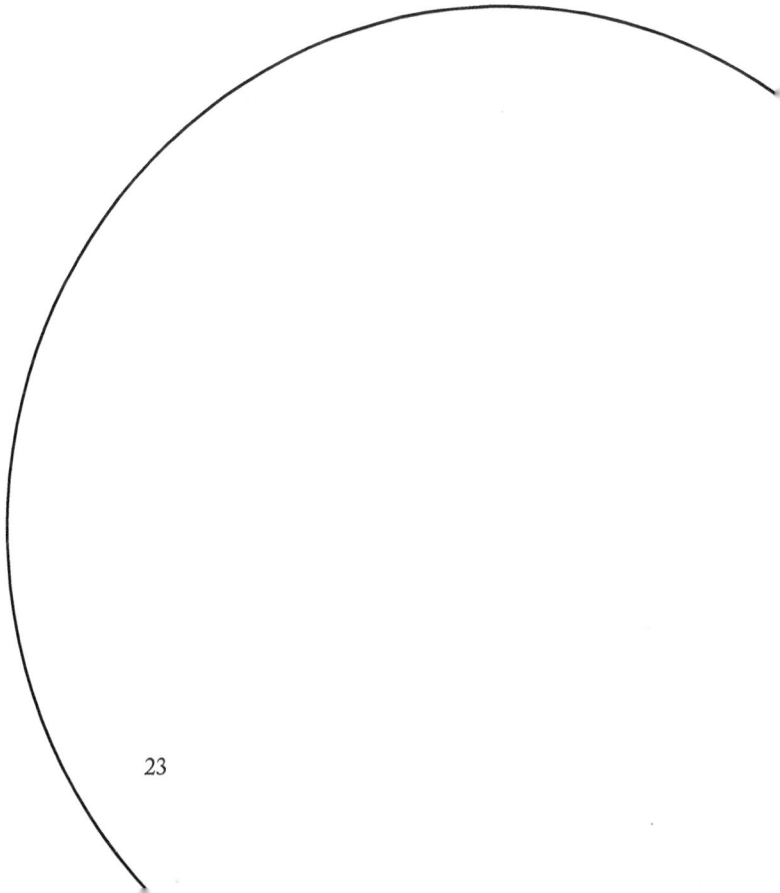

23

Whether a boundary is very small
or very large seems to be inconsequential.
So long as it is large or small enough
to elude the eye without the aid of instruments
these demarcations are sources of control.

A cell's organelles are organizational bodies.
Its DNA are its laws.

Like us, they simulate
a single being.

A cell can push us
through one way or another.

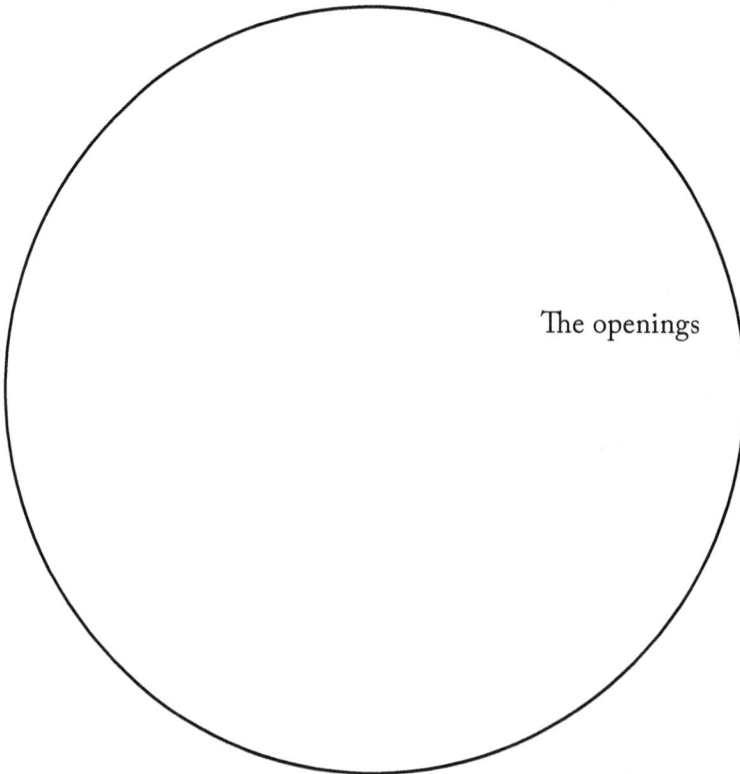

The openings   coax us inside.

How many folds will it take
to make you fit?

Cells build,
surround,
confine.

They are designed for us.
They possess a membrane
with enzymatic openings

which are the perfect
shapes for us.

(Question Set)

Is it the more you follow
the smaller you get?

and / or

The smaller you get
the more you need a Keeper?

and / or

Is there anything outside this?
If you see anything can you let me know?

III.

What Keeps the Winged Things

(They Say Please)

Organize yourselves. Keeper says the hardest part
is keeping the bees in place. He says their winged bodies

are perennially blooming. If it rains they may swarm
—God knows what else incurs their violence.

He says, *give them shelter, watch them leave.*
The Queen fulfills her body with indifferent duty.

She follows her most chemical senses
and senses what Keeper takes is taken willingly.

Soon, he will pluck her swollen body from the nuc
before she proves her fertile worth. The ability

to withhold the urge to seek another hive or naked
branch only increases her merit. Red is the color

of the year and it is brushed across her back:
it makes it easier for them to find each other.

The desire to be contained rises in bold crescendo now
above the chemical noise of gardenia:

the cicadas screaming into summer, full swing.

(According to Whom)

Keeper says seasonal optimization of bodies
is necessary in the early spring. He will ship swarms,

hundreds of thousands of winged bodies to brush
violence with their puberulous husks. Losing

a Queen is not a cheap risk. Like the bees,
a body of Keepers work together—a superorganism

that senses adversity, conjoined by an urge for containment
and willful mass dis-organization. He promises

our gums will numb from all toothaches,
for all the gold. The urge, if not for gold, then for

what? The winged keep working to increase their Keepers'
belly loads and the growers' sweep across the horizon,

ever fuller. Tracing gold upwards, othering to showcase
prosperity. Though the loss is also water, they drain

the drying earth until even it refuses the cicada-like clang
-clang of money. That's when need comes down swinging,

a velvet cushion, an amber-colored bruise.

(Dis-organization)

a a ability above according
across adversity all also
amber an and another are
back be bees bees before
belly blooming bodies body
bold branch bruise brush
brushed by cheap chemical
cicada-like cicadas clang-
clang color colored comes
conjoined contained
containment crescendo
cushion desire dis-
organization down drain
drying duty each early earth
easier else even ever fertile
find follows for from fulfills
full fuller gardenia give god
gold gold growers' gums

hardest he he her hive
horizon hundreds
husks if if in increase
increases incurs indifferent
into is it keep keeper keeper's
keepers keeping knows leave
like loads losing loss makes
mass may merit money most
naked necessary need noise
not now nuc numb of only
optimization or organize
other othering our part
perennially place please
pluck promises prosperity
proves puberulous queen
rains red refuses rises risk say
says says screaming seasonal
seek sense senses she she

shelter ship showcase
soon spring summer
superorganism swarm
swarms sweep swing
swinging swollen taken
takes that that's the the their
them then they
though thousands to together
toothache tracing
until upwards urge urge us
velvet violence watch water
what when will willful
willingly winged with
withhold work working
worth year yourselves

(Organization)

blooming
        bodies
each early earth
promises

(Re-organization)

The plan is already in place.

Keeper says the hardest part is keeping
the bees in place. Above the chemical noise
of gardenia, the cicadas are perennially blooming.

*

If it rains they may swarm,
or she fulfills her duty with an indifferent body.

Give them shelter, watch them leave.

*

He says the Queen, her back,
the thing which makes it easier
for them to find ——her,
her fertile worth—

her ability to withhold the urge to break
from the hive is her merit.

But red is the color of the year.

*

Red is brushed across her back—or God knows what
else incurs their violence.

Keeper then plucks her swollen body from the nucleus
of bee-made cells before she proves herself

screaming into a summer, full swing.

*

The smaller you get
the easier you are to push

into one cell or another.
The more singular, the easier

thinking you are alone,
(read: powerless.) And yet in numbers,

we rise, a violent, puberulous,
glistening swarm. We take over

the horizon's empty blue pull.
The bee does not see herself

as a single point among
thousands of other points.

She places herself among
Seurat's brushstrokes:

part of a dynamic whole.

(Cell 0)

This is the land of the beekeeper,
bound to the farm by his visa,

docile, unbarbed. The work of staying
in this country, making honey,

that is, is nothing
compared to selling Queens.

The Keeper has a keeper, too.
His keeper holds his visa, high up,

but he gives them shelter, a single
house on the apiary's property.

He tells me, when they swarm
it is near impossible

to catch them.
It is far easier to coerce them

using the grayish smoke
that blocks their natural inclinations.

Within a certain radius of us, the bees
are used for various corporate purposes.

And there are backyard keepers, too,
in the sprawl of suburbia surrounding us.

But only Keepers with a capital K
pluck the Queens before fertilization

to cage them for sale.
Still, he brings me their sweet

makings from the coastal mangroves:
saw palmetto, gallberry, orange blossom,

in thick glass jars.

IV.

The Superorganism

A.

Afghanistan

Venom is a marketable product. Keepers build an immunity to the bees here. Allowing themselves to be stung, they smile for the camera as if nothing is happening. In another village, children are taught apiculture. Keepers wear rubber gloves. Another town: women make up half of all Keepers. This is aid. As if nothing is happening, they need the money.

Albania

Algeria

Andorra

Angola

Antigua and Barbuda

Argentina

Armenia

Australia

Austria

Azerbaijan

B.

Bahamas

Exotic hives were introduced to the Bahamas as late as 1944. Previously,
Columbus arrived gold-hungry and in need of bodies. Seeing himself as a man
from the Heavens, he descended on the island he called San Salvador
and sent the natives to where he thought they came from.

Bahrain

Bangladesh

Barbados

Belarus

Belgium

Belize

Benin

Bhutan

Bolivia

Bosnia and Herzegovina

Botswana

Brazil

Brunei

Bulgaria

Burkina Faso Buru

Burundi

C.

Cambodia

There was no commercialization of hives here until the 1900s. Although honey and wax were exported and the bee larvae also eaten, honey-hunters harvested only what was needed and kept the open hives intact. This practice formed a symbiotic relationship in which no protective equipment was needed.

Cabo Verde

Cambodia

Cameroon

Canada

Central African Republic

Chad

Chile

China

Colombia

Comoros

Congo, Democratic Republic of the

Costa Rica

Côte d'Ivoire

Croatia

Cuba Cyprus

Czech Republic

D.

Denmark

Danefae once meant property of death. In the medieval era, this
meant anything not owned by an individual or forfeited by death
was property of the King. As for the bees, those whose swarms
had trespassed into others' lands were encouraged to share their gifts.
Present day: *Danefae* means a popular children's clothing brand.

Djibouti

Dominica

Dominican Republic

E.

East Timor

Ecuador

An article on the internet names the town of Cotocachi
a paradise at the end of a rainbow, citing a sign that states

God is here.

&

"Where else can you pop in for a shamanic cleansing
as if you were going to the dry cleaner's?"

Back in the US, Chicago kids start a fund to help raise money
for Andean students interested in supporting their villages
by selling honey and wax, the currency of the bees.

Egypt

El Salvador

Equatorial Guinea

Eritrea

Estonia

Eswatini

Ethiopia

F.

Fiji

Santalum album, more commonly known as sandalwood,
was the initial reason for commercial interest in the archipelago.
A shipwrecked sailor from an American ship sailing from Australia
depleted the sacred supply in less than twenty years.
But the bees are thriving, a triumph crafted by Keepers' choice
of Italian bees for their docility, the way they cling to the comb.

Finland

France

G.

Gabon

In the country of the holy wood, Tabernanthe iboga, drug tourism reigns.
For less than $1,000 you can experience a traditional Bwiti initiation rite,
a vacation package complete with a three day ibogaine trip to unknown ancestral lands.
The bees here, too, are used as currency, bodies governed by federal initiatives.
Nevertheless, when the Nganga leads the dance, sparks fly from both hemispheres.

Gambia, The

Georgia

Germany

Ghana

Greece

Grenada

Guatemala

Guinea

Guinea-Bissau

Guyana

H.

Haiti

According to the USAID website, political destabilization in the 1980s
led to the destruction of beekeepers' livelihoods and subsequently a shortage
of honey. USAID volunteers taught Haitian Keepers the importance
of confinement— the bees' need for structure in the flowerless months.

Honduras

Hungary

I.

Iceland

Keepers in Reykjavík struggle to keep their bees alive in the long winter. Swarm time comes as late as August. Bees are not native to the arctic, and so, if they survive, do well in the absence of disease, mites, foulbrood, and viruses commonly found in the tropics. Keepers are innovative, too, where keeping is not currency. If the environment is rich—if the larvae are fed with jelly— Keepers and bees are brought together against the elements.

India

Indonesia

Iran

Iraq

Ireland

Israel

Italy

J.

Jamaica

Keeper reminds us that there are stingless bees.
Edward Long, the author of the questionable *The History of Jamaica*,
whose chapter on the topographical conditions of the island
states that it is divided into three counties—Middlesex, Surry,
and Cornwall—describes the island honey's superiority
to the European variety while maintaining the general belief
that the enslaved population lacked something he called "genius."

Japan

Jordan

K.

Kazakhstan

Here there is no record of hive keeping before the 1770s. Before
the introduction of hives by descendants of the Russian Orthodox Church,
there were honey-hunters but no Keepers. Now, reporters forecast a boom
as demands for honey from neighboring China leaves locals scrambling
to split their hives or be left out of their own sweetness.

Kenya

Kiribati

Korea, North

Korea, South

Kosovo

Kuwait

Kyrgyzstan

L.

Laos

Apis cerana is kept in small hollowed trunks fortified at the end of the rainy season. This is a new development. There is little information on historical Keeping here. Open hives line branches of trees like little free arcs or wings. Still, when hunters here take, they destroy the hive in its entirety.

Latvia

Lebanon

Lesotho

Liberia

Libya

Liechtenstein

Lithuania

Luxembourg

M.

Madagascar

Malawi

Malaysia

Maldives

Mali

Malta

Marshall Islands

Mauritania

Mauritius

Mexico

Micronesia, Federated States of

Moldova

Monaco

Mongolia

Montenegro

Morocco

Mozambique

Myanmar (Burma)

N.

Namibia

In the Namibian newspaper, there is an article titled,
"Save the Bees, Get Free Honey," which is a feel-good story
about a Keeper that removes swarms trapped in houses and office buildings
to harvest the honey found therein. Keeper then shares this honey
with the human inhabitants of these spaces. He urges readers not to exterminate
bees, for we all have specific roles within our ecosystems.

Nauru

Nepal

Netherlands

New Zealand

Nicaragua

Niger

Nigeria

North Macedonia

Norway

O.

Oman

Keepers without protective gear use smoke made from the root
of the usbuq tree to calm the bees. They gently pull out a round
honeycomb disc and harvest the blood-colored honey.
Other Keepers use palette knives to scrape teardrop combs
filled with more honey than combs made by other bees,
taking great care not to disturb sleepy buzzers nearby.

P.

Pakistan

PARC, the Pakistan Agricultural Research Council,
promotes Keeping Apis mellifera or "European" bees.
The government employs those interested in the bee-saving process.
By teaching the art of Keeping as income to those living
in rural areas, Keepers become savers. Proudly, they share
how many hives have been created by this merger.

Palau

Panama

Q.

Qatar

In Qatar, a wealthy country, the term Beekeeper
refers to a phone application created by Hyatt Hotels.
Management uses it to communicate with their employees.
Beekeeper's main goal is to give orders to shift workers
who do not have steady access to a computer or email
throughout the day (such as housekeepers or janitorial staff).
It also helps track employee "engagement."

R.

Romania

Migrant Keepers drive mobile hives around the countryside.
Each cart has its own personality—a bright green one resembles
a barn; one looks like an apartment style mailbox kiosk on wheels.
Another, presumably from a highly successful Keeper, is a converted RV.
Video footage from a Keeper in Beregsău Mare states their mobile hive
houses over "one hundred families."

Russia

Rwanda

S.

Saint Kitts and Nevis

Saint Lucia

Saint Vincent and the Grenadines Samoa

San Marino

Sao Tome and Principe

Saudi Arabia

Senegal

Serbia

Seychelles

Sierra Leone

Singapore

Slovakia

Slovenia

Solomon Islands

Somalia

South Africa

Spain

Sri Lanka

Sudan

Sudan, South

Suriname

Sweden

Switzerland

Syria

T.

Taiwan

In Taipei, Keepers participating in the first urban keeping project
can't help but press their fingers into sticky combs. A young woman
wearing a thin veil explains that the species of plants native
to the area are still diverse enough to create high quality honey.
She allows a few bees to land on her hands before gently blowing them away.

Tajikistan

Tanzania

Thailand

Tibet

Togo

Tonga

Trinidad and Tobago

Tunisia

Turkey

Turkmenistan

Tuvalu

U.

Uganda

Keeping is a governmental initiative for poverty reduction wherein Keepers use traditional log hives newly outfitted with corrugated roofs.

Ukraine

United Arab Emirates

United Kingdom

United States

Uruguay

Uzbekistan

V.

Vanuatu

Keepers build special houses to protect the bees from climate change.
Seeing potential for profit, an expat Keeper creates several innovations
for keeping hives cooler in rising temperatures. Hives are upgraded
to wire mesh flooring and are enclosed in bee "houses,"
keeping out the sun and wind.

Vatican City

Venezuela

Vietnam

W.

X.

Y.

Yemen

Beehives are kept in dry river beds. There are two types:
wooden tubes and pottery. USAID calls honey "Yemen's Liquid Gold."
They state their aim is to tap into honey production as a means of driving profit
for the rural population. Women are encouraged to Keep, construct, and harvest.

Z.

Zambia

Traditional bark tree hives are the norm. Aid programs seeking
to alleviate poverty teach new Keepers to profit from these traditions,
as opposed to building western-style removable frame hives.
Keeping has a long history here. There is a cultural connection
to the business of translating sweetness into cash.

Zimbabwe

V.

Instruction Set / If

(Instruction)

it's not about one hive or a lack of hive
to invade a human: invade a human sized hive

size up the animal in question
then split the organism

bonus: split hive again

(Inequality I)

This cell is larger
than anything
we can see.

≠

Healing cannot be
produced by a single
member of the colony.

(Tentative Instruction)

can we loom larger than
the horizon so large

we seem flat

can we extend beyond it
can you tell me

is there always another wall
behind another wall

is this what is called
an institution?

(Inequality II)

How they sting
as they get loaded onto
west-bound trucks.

≠

How we sing
as they get loaded onto
west-bound trucks.

(Reverse Instruction)

are you a part of this hive or a better question is
should you be

a sadder question is are you allowed here
do you fit this particular compartment

did you check all the necessary boxes
have you asked the necessary questions

to pass through this membranous sheath
into another membranous sheath

into another membranous sheath

have you sat in a particular room
with other particular beings

and for how long
and why

do you inhabit a certain color or shape
how long do you sit here

and try like a virus to fit
and how many cell walls are there anyway

I can't see

how long before the colony up & quits?

(Inequality III)

We worked outdoors.

We did not understand
their swarm is not an attack.

≠

We did not understand—
who are the attackers?

Whose capture is imminent?

(Necessary Instruction)

consider the names of those who design
each cell's permeability

tell your neighbor

(Inequality IV)

Can nurturing only be done
on a case-by-case basis?

$\neq$

Can we can save the colony
by failing commercially?

(Instruction)

it's not about one hive or
a lack of hive

inspect the hive for brood rot

apply terramycin
wait wait

don't disturb healthy larvae
pearly, white, glistening

they have not yet awoken

(Inequality V)

Keeper promises
to set us free.

≠

The othering is meant to
showcase prosperity.

(If)

If this book, page, sentence, word, letter, space is

If this music, sound, phoneme, wave is

If this kernel of thought diffuses
       from one body into another

If electric impulses are translated
       from invisible light into ink

If photons reach retina, cones, neurons

If you begin to feel like part of a whole
       without becoming infinitesimal, unseen

If it no longer matters to be
       quiet, compliant

    then

About the Author

Lucianna Chixaro Ramos is a Brazilian-born poet. She works as a graphic designer and is an advocate for a child's right to safety. Lucianna is a graduate of Stetson University's MFA of the Americas. You can find more of her work in print and online in the journals *New South, Bombay Gin, Anastamos*, and elsewhere.

Acknowledgements

Versions of "(They Say Please)," "(According to Whom)," and "(Cell 0)" appeared in a digital issue of *Fantastic Floridas*.

Early versions of "(Afghanistan - Bahamas)," "(Egypt - France)," "(Gabon - Haiti)," "(Holy See - Jamaica)," and "(Japan - Koreas)" appeared on Volume 8, Issue 3 of *After the Pause*.

This work was discussed at length in the podcast "Out of Print" with publisher Ryan Rivas in 2017.

Many poems in this collection borrow from Robert Hooke's *Micrographia*. In many cases these excerpts are signaled by italics.

I am ever grateful to the constellation of beings at the MFA of the Americas at Stetson University, including Terri Witek, Jena Osman, Urayoán Noel, Cyriaco Lopes, Laura Mullen, and others that provided advice during the early stages of this project.

Forever indebted to my fellow poets who never tired of the buzzing (or hid it exceptionally well): Jacklyn Gion, Jennifer Paccione, and many others.